D1254086

First published by Fiona Reeves on Amazon Kindle in 2015

Text Copyright © 2015 Fiona Reeves.
Illustrations Copyright © 2015 Billy Allison.

ISBN: 1517038677
ISBN-13: 978-1517038670

For Thomas and his sister Erin. I love you!

- Fiona

Acknowledgements

Thank you to Nisha Frizzell and Allison Foreman for reading my early drafts and providing helpful feedback and suggestions. Thank you to my husband Mark Reeves for checking over and helping with the final version.

Special thank you to Billy Allison for turning my idea scribbles into beautiful professional illustrations.

Contents

The children's guide to Autism

FIONA REEVES

ILLUSTRATED BY BILLY ALLISON

different brains

Every person is different. They like different things and they behave differently. They think different thoughts.

Your brain controls how you think and feel and move. Every person is different because we all have different brains, but they usually work in nearly the same way.

People with something called Autism have brains that work more differently to other people. That isn't bad, it's just different. They were born with brains that work differently and will always have brains that work differently. It is not the same as being ill.

the autism spectrum

Every person with Autism is different. That's why it's called a spectrum. The Autism Spectrum. For example some people with Autism might not speak at all, and other people with Autism can speak amazingly well.

Some people with Autism will find things difficult that most people find easy, like brushing their hair. They might also find things easy that most people find difficult.

understanding people

People with Autism can find it hard to understand body language or know how somebody else is feeling, for example whether they are happy, sad, scared, excited, interested or bored. They can also find it difficult to know and understand the usual thing to say or do in a situation.

They might say or do something that is surprising and unexpected to other people because their thoughts and feelings work differently, or they don't understand what's happening around them. This can make other people think they are 'odd' and not want to spend time with them, which is sad because people with Autism love to have friends, but their Autism makes it difficult to make friendships.

People with Autism usually make very honest and loyal friends.

the right words

When asking a person with Autism a question, think about the words you use, because they will answer exactly the question you ask.

If you ask them "would you like to play football?" they might answer "no" because they don't want to play football at the moment, but if you had asked "would you like to come and play with us?" they might have answered "yes".

They are honest about how they are feeling. Next time you ask they might be ready, so don't give up asking!

communicating

A person with Autism might take a long time to think about what you have said to them before they answer, so be patient and wait.

They might talk for a long time about something they really like (for example trains, natural disasters, Minecraft), or they might repeat something they've heard in a film or read in a book or even that you have said to them.

noticing details

Some people with Autism have amazingly detailed memories.

They can remember every word said in a whole film they've only seen once and can repeat it all, or remember a book they read a year ago, or they might remember something they've seen so well that they can draw every single detail accurately from their memory.

senses

For most people with Autism, their senses can play tricks on them. A room might look a lot smaller than it is. They might hear a sound a lot louder, or a lot quieter, than other people. They might talk loudly or shout a lot (if they hear things quietly then they need to make more noise). A gentle touch might feel painful, or a hard hit might feel soft. A smell, taste or texture might be upsetting. They might like to chew things.

When their senses play tricks on them it can make them feel bad, they might feel scared or trapped and need to escape. They might shout, hit, try to hide or cover their ears. They could flap their hands or make rhythmic movements like rocking to try to comfort themselves. Making humming noises might help block out the other scary senses. If it all gets too much their brain might just shut down for a while for a rest.

Busy, noisy places can be very difficult for someone with Autism. It also makes it difficult to realise when someone is calling your name, or trying to talk to you.

It can be difficult to get the attention of someone with Autism to tell them something, particularly if there is a lot going on around them.

If someone with Autism is struggling with a noisy and busy place then try to help them to get to somewhere quieter, you could ask an adult to help.

coping with change

Things changing from the way they are normally done can be difficult and scary for someone on the Autism spectrum. Travelling in a different car, going swimming in the morning instead of the afternoon or being collected from school by a different person could be distressing.

People with Autism like to know what is going to happen later in the day so that they are prepared for it and it is not a surprise. Liking things to be done the same way can also mean that sometimes they expect games to be played in exactly the same way every time and can get upset if that doesn't happen.

difference is great!

We need everybody in the world to be different, so that there are different ideas. Some people with Autism are amazing scientists, their different way of thinking lets them think of brilliant new ideas for explaining how the universe works.

Every person has things they are good at and things they need help with, whether they have Autism or not.

Now you know what can be difficult for someone with Autism, and why, it will help you to understand them. Be patient and kind, and think of ways to help them when you see that they are struggling, or invite them to join in your game if they come and say something to you or give you something.

finding out more

Resources for finding out more about Autism.

The National Autistic Society (UK)
www.autism.org.uk

Leisure for Autism (UK)
www.leisureforautism.org

The Autism Discussion Page
https://www.facebook.com/autismdiscussionpage

about the author

Fiona Reeves lives in Manchester, UK with her husband Mark and two children Erin and Thomas. Thomas was diagnosed with Autism when he was 6 years old, and he loves reading.

Fiona wrote this book to explain Thomas's Autism to him and his friends in a factual way rather than a story about a specific character with very specific symptoms, as Autism isn't like that. Fiona has primarily worked as a Software Engineer and Website Developer.

www.fionareeves.co.uk

about the illustrator

Billy Allison lives with his lovely wife Shelly and their two sons Clay and Taylor. He is an experienced artist who has primarily worked in the animation industry and has also spent time working in the games world. In animation he has worked on many TV series and commercials and animated various pilot projects.

www.blimation.com

Made in the USA
San Bernardino, CA
25 February 2020